TEAM SPIRIT ®

SMART BOOKS FOR YOUNG FANS

30▶ 20▶ 10▶

THE MIAMI DOLPHINS

BY
MARK STEWART

NORWOOD HOUSE PRESS
CHICAGO, ILLINOIS

Norwood House Press
P.O. Box 316598
Chicago, Illinois 60631

For information regarding Norwood House Press, please visit our website at:
www.norwoodhousepress.com or call 866-565-2900.

Editor: Mike Kennedy
Designer: Ron Jaffe
Project Management: Black Book Partners, LLC.
Special thanks to Topps, Inc.

Library of Congress Cataloging-in-Publication Data

Stewart, Mark, 1960-
    The Miami Dolphins / by Mark Stewart.
       p. cm. -- (Team spirit)
    Includes bibliographical references and index.
    Summary: "Team Spirit Football edition featuring the Miami Dolphins that
chronicles the history and accomplishments of the team. Includes access to
the Team Spirit website which provides additional information and
photos"--Provided by publisher.
    ISBN 978-1-59953-528-9 (library edition : alk. paper) -- ISBN
978-1-60357-470-9 (ebook)
    1. Miami Dolphins (Football team)--History--Juvenile literature. I.
Title.
    GV956.M47S74 2012
    796.332'6409759381--dc23
                                                    2012012645

Manufactured in the United States of America in North Mankato, Minnesota.
205N—082012

COVER PHOTO: The Dolphins take the field before a game.

Table of Contents

ABOUT OUR GLOSSARY

In this book, there may be several words that you are reading for the first time. Some are sports words, some are new vocabulary words, and some are familiar words that are used in an unusual way. All of these words are defined on page 46. Throughout the book, sports words appear in **bold type**. Regular vocabulary words appear in *bold italic type*.

Meet the Dolphins

You could travel to every corner of the United States, but it is unlikely you would find a place with more *diversity* than Miami, Florida. People of all ages and backgrounds live there. They love the area's warm beaches, sunny days, tasty food, and fun music. They also love getting together with friends on Sundays in the fall to watch the Dolphins.

The Dolphins have played in Miami longer than any other *professional* team there. Yet they are still young compared to teams in many other cities. In fact, thousands of fans who followed the Dolphins in their first season still go to see them play today.

This book tells the story of the Dolphins. Although the team has had many stars over the years, Miami fans know that winning often depends on players who are on the field for only a few downs a game. For the Dolphins, teamwork is the name of the game.

The Dolphins celebrate a scoring play during the 2011 season. When Miami plays together as one, the results are amazing.

Glory Days

During the 1960s, the **American Football League (AFL)** and the older **National Football League (NFL)** competed for players and fans. Both leagues set their sights on the South, where college football was already very popular. They believed that professional football would do well there, too.

A businessman named Joe Robbie was eager to start a team of his own. The AFL suggested that he place his team in Miami. The city's population had doubled in a *generation*. There were new fans being born every day! Robbie liked what he saw. The Dolphins played their first season in 1966.

The Dolphins built their team by selecting players from other AFL clubs. They also found college stars in the **draft**. But Miami struggled in its first season and won just three games. The Dolphins had so many injured quarterbacks that coach George Wilson ended up using his son to call the signals!

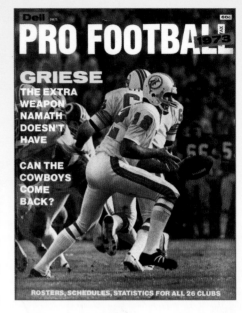

Over the next few years, the Dolphins put together a group of good young players, including Bob Griese, Larry Csonka, Howard Twilley, Dick Anderson, Jim Kiick, and Mercury Morris. Miami also traded for older stars, such as Nick Buoniconti, Paul Warfield, and Bob Matheson. In 1970—the year that the AFL and NFL joined forces—the team hired Don Shula as its coach. In only his second season, the Dolphins made it to the **Super Bowl**!

Before long, Miami became one of the best teams in history. They returned to the Super Bowl twice during the 1970s and took the championship both times. In 1972, the Dolphins won all 14 games during the regular season. They added three more **postseason** victories—including Super Bowl VII—to become the first NFL team to finish with a perfect 17–0 record.

The Dolphins succeeded because everyone on the team worked hard and did his job well. Most football fans in the 1970s

LEFT: Don Shula directs his players.   **ABOVE**: Bob Griese and the Dolphins were on a lot of magazine covers in the 1970s.

did not know much about players such as Jim Langer, Larry Little, Bob Kuechenberg, Manny Fernandez, Bill Stanfill, and Vern Den Herder. But Miami's opponents sure knew who they were.

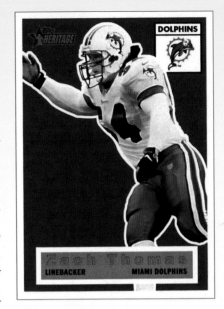

The same was true years later, when the Dolphins were led by A.J. Duhe, Bob Baumhower, Dwight Stephenson, Ed Newman, Duriel Harris, Andra Franklin, and David Woodley. They were champions of the **American Football Conference (AFC)** in 1982, but they lost to the Washington Redskins in Super Bowl XVII.

The Dolphins hoped that a new quarterback would change their luck. They found one in strong-armed Dan Marino, who led them back to the Super Bowl. During his long and brilliant career, Marino smashed almost every NFL passing record.

Shula retired in 1996, and Marino did the same four seasons later. The Dolphins found new leaders in a pair of defensive stars, Zach Thomas and Jason Taylor. Both were hard workers who got the job done without being flashy. They *inspired* their teammates to give everything they had on every play.

LEFT: Dan Marino loosens up before a game.
ABOVE: This trading card shows linebacker Zack Thomas in action.

Taylor and Thomas led the Dolphins as Miami rebuilt for the 21st century. Among Miami's stars during this time were quarterbacks Jay Fiedler and Chad Pennington, receivers Chris Chambers and Brandon Marshall, and running backs Ricky Williams and Ronnie Brown.

With so many new faces moving in and out of the lineup, the Dolphins had good years and bad years. They won their **division** in 2000 and 2001. Those teams relied on a strong defense that attacked opponents from all angles. But in 2007, Miami won just one game. It was the worst season in team history.

The following year, Miami went 11–5 and returned to the **playoffs**. Linebacker Joey Porter terrorized quarterbacks all season long with 17.5 **sacks**. Williams and Brown formed a great one-two punch running the ball. Pennington rarely made a mistake

throwing the ball. The 2008 season showed how tiny the difference is between winning and losing in the NFL.

The Dolphins know what it takes to build a championship squad. They start with exciting players such as Jake Long, Reggie Bush, and Cameron Wake. Then the team fills out its roster with role players who do exactly what is asked of them. Miami begins each season expecting to reach the playoffs and compete for a spot in the Super Bowl. And who knows? Maybe the Dolphins will go undefeated again. If it happened once, it can happen again!

LEFT: Ronnie Brown ran for more than 1,000 yards in his first NFL season.
ABOVE: Cameron Wake takes on a blocker.

Home Turf

For many years, the Dolphins played their home games in Miami's Orange Bowl. In 1987, the team opened a stadium in Miami Gardens, which is a suburb of the city. The stadium has gone through many different names. At one point, it was called Joe Robbie Stadium, after the team's first owner.

The Dolphins' stadium is one of the most *luxurious* sports arenas in the United States. It has hosted the Super Bowl five times and many other important sports events. Every seat in the stadium has a great view of the field. If fans happen to miss a play, they can always watch an instant replay on one of two huge video scoreboards located at each end of the field.

BY THE NUMBERS

- The Dolphins' stadium has 75,192 seats.
- The stadium has been used to host the Super Bowl five times.
- In all, the stadium has more than 2,000 flat-screen TV monitors, including several 103-inch plasma displays.

This picture shows the Dolphins' stadium before Super Bowl XXIX between the San Diego Chargers and San Francisco 49ers.

Dressed for Success

The uniforms the Dolphins wore in their first season were very similar to the ones they use today. The team's colors are aqua green, coral orange, blue, and white. These colors remind people of the ocean and warm weather.

So does the team *logo*. It shows a dolphin in front of an orange sunburst. The Miami helmet is white, with green and orange stripes running down the middle and the logo on each side. Like the Dolphins' uniform, it has changed very little over the years.

In 2003, the Dolphins introduced coral orange jerseys for home games. They wear these on special occasions. Normally, the team dresses in either its green jerseys or white jerseys for home games.

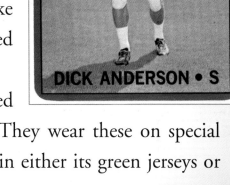

DICK ANDERSON • S

LEFT: The Dolphins' famous logo can be seen on Jason Taylor's helmet and jersey.   **ABOVE**: Dick Anderson poses for this 1972 trading card in the team's aqua green jersey.

We Won!

In the NFL, it usually takes many years for a new team to reach the Super Bowl. But the Dolphins did things differently. In 1971, in just the team's sixth year, Miami had its second winning season. Fans didn't expect much in the playoffs because the Dolphins were

matched against opponents with much more experience. But they defeated the Kansas City Chiefs and the Baltimore Colts in two exciting games to reach Super Bowl VI. The Dolphins met the Dallas Cowboys but lost 24–3.

The following season, the Dolphins were the team with Super Bowl experience. They showed it by going through the entire regular season without losing a single game. After quarterback Bob Griese broke his leg early in the year, coach Don Shula convinced his players that they

could still win without their leader. Shula turned to 38-year-old Earl Morrall to take the snaps, and the Dolphins continued to pile up victory after victory.

After finishing the regular season at 14–0, Miami defeated the Cleveland Browns and Pittsburgh Steelers in thrilling playoff games. Griese returned from his injury in time to lead the Dolphins into Super Bowl VII against the Washington Redskins.

The Dolphins had three excellent runners in Larry Csonka, Jim Kiick, and Mercury Morris. What made the team great, however, was its "No Name" defense. Manny Fernandez, Nick Buoniconti, and Jake Scott led the unit, which got its nickname because most fans outside of Florida were unfamiliar with the Miami players.

In the Super Bowl, the Dolphins stopped Washington cold. The Redskins struggled to make first downs, and the offense went the entire game without scoring a **field goal** or touchdown. Their only points came on a defensive play late in the game.

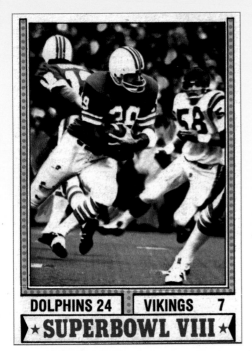

DOLPHINS 24 | **VIKINGS 7**
★ **SUPERBOWL VIII** ★

The Dolphins, meanwhile, moved the ball *consistently* up and down the field. Griese threw a touchdown pass to Howard Twilley, and Kiick scored on a short run. Miami won 14–7. Scott, who **intercepted** two passes, was named the game's **Most Valuable Player (MVP)**. The Dolphins had made history as the NFL's first undefeated team.

Miami returned to the Super Bowl a year later. After posting a 12–2 record, the Dolphins beat the Cincinnati Bengals and Oakland Raiders in the playoffs. Just as they had the year before, the Dolphins used their running game to wear down their opponents, while the defense gave up few points.

In Super Bowl VIII, Miami faced the Minnesota Vikings. Both teams had great defenses. But Csonka was the difference-maker for Miami. He put his head down and plowed his way to 145 yards and two touchdowns. Minnesota's star running back, Chuck Foreman, didn't fare nearly as well. He gained just 18 yards against the No Names. The Dolphins rolled to a 24–7 victory and their second championship in a row.

Miami fans believed their team would win many more Super Bowls. Although the Dolphins returned to the big game twice more, they did not find the championship magic again. In Super Bowl XVII—a rematch with the Redskins—the Dolphins were ahead 13–10 in the fourth quarter, but they could not hold the lead. In Super Bowl XIX, Dan Marino and Joe Montana of the San Francisco 49ers each passed for more than 300 yards, but Miami fell 38–16.

Were the Dolphins of the early 1970s the greatest team ever? Many football experts believe that they were. The team went a combined 32–2 in 1972 and 1973. And when the Dolphins played in the Super Bowl, they won with *dominant* performances.

LEFT: This trading card celebrates Miami's win in Super Bowl VIII.
ABOVE: Paul Warfield and Garo Yepremian remind today's fans that only one team has gone unbeaten through an entire season.

Go-To Guys

To be a true star in the NFL, you need more than fast feet and a big body. You have to be a "go-to guy"—someone the coach wants on the field at the end of a big game. Dolphins fans have had a lot to cheer about over the years, including these great stars …

THE PIONEERS

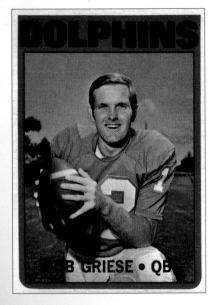

BOB GRIESE   Quarterback

- BORN: 2/3/1945   • PLAYED FOR TEAM: 1967 TO 1980

Bob Griese was one of the most reliable quarterbacks ever. He was a smart leader and an accurate passer who understood how to use all of Miami's weapons. Griese was voted into the **Hall of Fame** in 1990.

LARRY CSONKA   Running Back

- BORN: 12/25/1946
- PLAYED FOR TEAM: 1968 TO 1974 & 1979

Larry Csonka could run around tacklers, but he preferred to run over them. The defensive players of the 1970s say that no one was harder to bring down. Csonka gained more than 1,000 yards in both of Miami's championship seasons.

NICK BUONICONTI   Linebacker

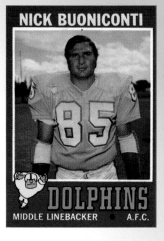

- BORN: 12/15/1940   • PLAYED FOR TEAM: 1969 TO 1974 & 1976

Nick Buoniconti was the heart of the No Name defense. He was a hard tackler who played like every down was his last. In 1973, he set a team record with 162 tackles.

LARRY LITTLE   Offensive Lineman

- BORN: 11/2/1945   • PLAYED FOR TEAM: 1969 TO 1980

Larry Little was the key blocker in Miami's rushing attack. He was strong enough to push his man straight back on inside runs. He was also quick enough to pull around the end and lead the blocking on outside runs.

PAUL WARFIELD   Receiver

- BORN: 11/28/1942   • PLAYED FOR TEAM: 1970 TO 1974

Paul Warfield was Miami's most dangerous weapon. When opponents crowded the line to stop the run, Warfield would catch long passes to break open close games. He averaged more than 21 yards per reception.

BOB BAUMHOWER   Defensive Lineman

- BORN: 8/4/1955   • PLAYED FOR TEAM: 1977 TO 1986

Miami hit the jackpot when it picked Bob Baumhower and A.J. Duhe in the first round of the 1977 draft. They formed the heart of the team's top-ranked defense. Baumhower was picked to play in the **Pro Bowl** five times.

LEFT: Bob Griese   **ABOVE**: Nick Buoniconti

DWIGHT STEPHENSON   Center

- BORN: 11/20/1957   • PLAYED FOR TEAM: 1980 TO 1987

It took just one season for Dwight Stephenson to win a starting job with the Dolphins. When he was given a chance, he proved to be one of the best centers in history. He was voted **All-Pro** five years in a row.

MARK DUPER   Receiver

- BORN: 1/25/1959   • PLAYED FOR TEAM: 1982 TO 1992

Mark Duper had incredible speed. He often zoomed right past defensive backs on deep pass plays. He and Mark Clayton were nicknamed the "Marks Brothers." His best season came in 1986 when he averaged nearly 20 yards a catch and scored 11 touchdowns, including an 85-yarder.

MARK CLAYTON   Receiver

- BORN: 4/8/1961   • PLAYED FOR TEAM: 1983 TO 1992

Mark Clayton was quick and crafty. He was an expert at getting open, and few receivers were harder to tackle. In 1984, Clayton caught 18 touchdown passes.

DAN MARINO   Quarterback

- BORN: 9/15/1961   • PLAYED FOR TEAM: 1983 TO 1999

Many football experts consider Dan Marino to be the best quarterback ever. He released the ball so quickly and threw with such accuracy that he changed the way NFL defenses were designed. In 1984, Marino threw for 48 touchdowns and more than 5,000 yards.

RICHMOND WEBB — Offensive Lineman

• BORN: 1/11/1967   • PLAYED FOR TEAM: 1990 TO 2000

Richmond Webb's job was to protect Dan Marino. He set team records by starting in 118 games in a row and playing in seven straight Pro Bowls.

JASON TAYLOR — Defensive End

• BORN: 9/1/1974

• PLAYED FOR TEAM: 1997 TO 2007, 2009 & 2011

Jason Taylor loved playing for Miami. He had a special talent for getting to the quarterback. During his career, Taylor returned six **fumbles** for touchdowns— the most in NFL history.

JAKE LONG — Offensive Lineman

• BORN: 5/9/1985

• FIRST YEAR WITH TEAM: 2008

The Dolphins were so sure that Jake Long would become a star that they made him the first pick in the 2008 draft. Long lived up to their expectations. He was picked for the Pro Bowl in each of his first four seasons.

RIGHT: Jake Long

23

Calling the Shots

When Miami fans heard that the Dolphins had hired Don Shula to coach the team in 1970, they had a feeling that the team would improve quickly. He had led the Baltimore Colts to the Super Bowl two years earlier. The Dolphins had suffered through losing records in each of their first four seasons. Under Shula, they lost only four games in 1970 and made the playoffs. In 1971, they went to the Super Bowl. In 1972, they won the Super Bowl—and every other game they played that year!

In 26 years as coach, Shula had only two losing seasons. One reason for his success was that he made great use of every player on the team. In the 1970s, the Dolphins had good blockers and talented runners. So they ran the ball play after play until they wore down their opponents.

In the 1980s and 1990s, Shula did not have a running back who gained 1,000 yards. But his quarterback was Dan Marino, so the team won by passing the ball. Shula was never afraid to experiment and try something new. Playing the Dolphins was tough when he coached them because opponents never knew what to expect.

Don Shula discusses his game plan with Don Strock and Dan Marino.

In the years that followed, the Dolphins looked hard for a coach like Shula. They hired some of football's best minds, including Jimmy Johnson, Dave Wannstedt, and Nick Saban. Needless to say, each was under great pressure to live up to Shula's record of excellence, which was almost impossible to do.

In 2012, the Dolphins hired Joe Philbin to coach the team. He had helped the Green Bay Packers return to the top of the NFL. Miami fans hoped he would do the same for the Dolphins.

One Great Day

When Dolphins fans settled in front of their televisions on Christmas Day in 1971, they were all wishing for the same gift: the team's first-ever playoff victory. It would not be easy. Miami faced the Kansas City Chiefs—the Super Bowl champions two years earlier—on the road.

Both teams had star-studded lineups. Everyone believed that the game would come down to a great play by Miami's Bob Griese or Jim Kiick, or by Kansas City's Len Dawson or Otis Taylor. No one expected the kickers to be the story. But Garo Yepremian of the Dolphins and Jan Stenerud of the Chiefs took center stage as the game progressed.

The Chiefs led 10–0 in the first quarter, but the Dolphins fought back to tie the score at halftime. Kansas City scored twice in the second half. Each time, Miami tied the game again. The Chiefs had a chance to win as time ran out, but Stenerud's kick sailed wide, and the game went into **overtime** knotted at 24–24.

Jim Kiick crosses the goal line for the Dolphins during their Christmas Day battle with the Kansas City Chiefs.

The Chiefs moved quickly to end the game, driving deep into Miami territory. Stenerud tried another field goal, but Nick Buoniconti saved the day by blocking the kick. Neither team scored during the 15-minute extra period, so for the first time in NFL history a game went into double overtime.

Finally, halfway through the second extra period, Miami drove to Kansas City's 30-yard line. Yepremian, the smallest player on the field, made the biggest kick of his life. His field goal tumbled over the crossbar to give the Dolphins a 27–24 victory in the longest game ever played.

Legend Has It

Who was the worst passer in Miami history?

LEGEND HAS IT that Garo Yepremian was. Of course, he was a kicker, so no one expected him to throw the ball. Toward the end of Super Bowl VII, Yepremian ran onto the field to try a field goal. But the kick was blocked, and the ball bounced right back to Yepremian. That's when he realized that the entire Washington defense was charging at him. Yepremian decided to attempt the first pass of his career. As his arm went forward, the ball popped straight in the air. Mike Bass of the Redskins caught it and ran 49 yards for a touchdown.

ABOVE: Garo Yepremian and holder Karl Noonan show how their

What was the team's most famous play?

LEGEND HAS IT that the "Hook & **Lateral**" was. In the 1981 playoffs, the Dolphins trailed the San Diego Chargers late in the second quarter. It looked like they wouldn't score again before halftime. But Don Shula had a trick up his sleeve. Duriel Harris ran a 20-yard "hook" pattern, and quarterback Don Strock fired a pass to him. With the defense moving to tackle him, Harris quickly pitched the ball to Tony Nathan, who was streaking down the field. Nathan blew past the Chargers and ran for a touchdown.

Who was the Dolphins' most talented couch potato?

LEGEND HAS IT that Cameron Wake was. Wake was a star linebacker in college, but he spent two years at home watching games on television before any pro team showed interest in him. He called himself a "couch potato." In 2007, Wake decided to play in the **Canadian Football League (CFL)**. After two seasons, he joined the Dolphins. In 2010, Wake had 14 sacks and became the star of the Miami defense.

It Really Happened

When the 1972 season began, the Dolphins had three of the best running backs in the NFL: Larry Csonka, Jim Kiick, and Mercury Morris. Csonka played fullback, while Morris and Kiick split time at halfback. Kiick saw more action than Morris, but when Morris carried the ball he often ran for big gains. The

Dolphins won game after game with their three stars and finished the regular season with a perfect 14–0 record.

After the final game, Csonka had 1,117 yards. It marked the second year in a row he had run for more than 1,000 yards. Morris finished with 991 yards. Or did he? Earlier in the season, Morris had dropped a short pass from Bob Griese.

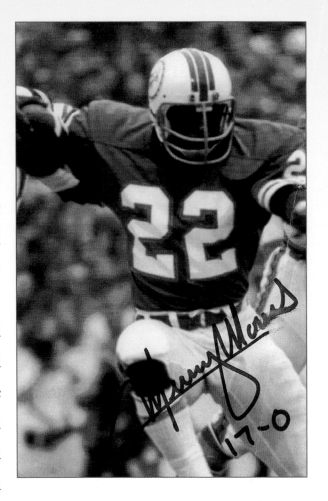

The play was ruled a fumble, because the referee believed the ball had gone backwards. That made the play a lateral, and Morris was charged with a loss of nine yards.

As the Dolphins prepared for the playoffs, the team called the NFL and asked the league to review the play. Film from that day was analyzed, and the NFL changed its call from a fumble to an incomplete pass. Morris was credited with the nine yards, giving him exactly 1,000 for the season.

That made Csonka and Morris the first teammates in history to run for 1,000 yards in the same season. Not surprisingly, Miami set a record that year by gaining 2,960 yards as a team. They averaged more than 200 yards a game on the ground!

Team Spirit

Miami may be home to warm weather and calming seas, but that doesn't mean that Dolphins fans are laid back. Ever since the team's perfect season in 1972, they have had very high expectations. If the team is not playing well, fans have been known to hold protests and demand more from the players and coaches.

The Dolphins appreciate the passion of their fans. They know that there are plenty of things to do in South Florida on a beautiful fall day. Winning is the easiest way to make sure all the seats in Miami's stadium are filled for every home game.

Win or lose, going to a Dolphins game is always entertaining. The team has one of the best cheerleading squads in the NFL. Fans also love the team mascot, T.D. His name is an abbreviation of "touchdown."

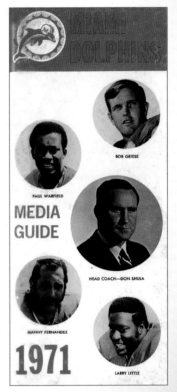

LEFT: Don Shula reunites with his 1972 players and their families.
ABOVE: This guide book covers the team's first AFC Championship season.

Timeline

In this timeline, each Super Bowl is listed under the year it was played. Remember that the Super Bowl is held early in the year and is actually part of the previous season. For example, Super Bowl XLVI was played on February 5, 2012, but it was the championship of the 2011 NFL season.

1966
The Dolphins play their first season.

1974
The Dolphins win their second Super Bowl.

1970
The Dolphins hire coach Don Shula.

1973
Miami wins Super Bowl VII to complete an undefeated 1972 season.

1983
The Dolphins win their fourth AFC championship.

Howard Twilley played for Miami in 1966 and also in three Super Bowls.

Paul Warfield helped the Dolphins win the Super Bowl twice.

PAUL WARFIELD

42

DOLPHINS

WIDE RECEIVER · ALL-STAR

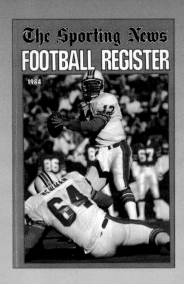

Dan
Marino

Cameron
Wake

1984
Dan Marino throws
48 touchdown passes.

1999
Olindo Mare
leads the NFL
with 39 field goals.

2010
Jake Long and
Cameron Wake
make the Pro Bowl.

1985
The Dolphins
return to the AFC
Championship Game.

2002
Jason Taylor leads
the NFL with
18.5 sacks.

2011
Reggie Bush runs
for 1,000 yards.

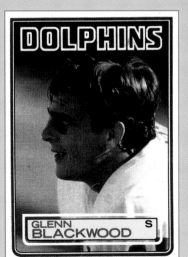

Glenn Blackwood led
the 1985 team with
six interceptions.

Fun Facts

LIGHT ON HIS FEET

In 2008, Jason Taylor competed on the television program *Dancing with the Stars*. He made it to the finals but finished second to Olympic figure skater Kristi Yamaguchi.

SACK MASTERS

In 1973, Bill Stanfill set a team record when he was credited with 18.5 sacks. Jason Taylor tied his mark in 2002.

ALL OR NOTHING

Linebacker Larry Ball is the only player in history to play for an undefeated team and a winless team. He was on the 17–0 Dolphins in 1972. Five years later, he played for the Tampa Bay Buccaneers when they went 0–14.

FAST FREDDIE

In a 1976 game, Freddie Solomon scored three touchdowns for the Dolphins—one on a 79-yard punt return, another on a 53-yard pass play, and another on a 59-yard run.

FOUR SCORE

In the Pro Bowl after the 2011 season, Brandon Marshall scored four touchdowns. That set a record for the annual game.

NAME GAME

In a contest to name the team in 1965, Dolphins just beat Sharks to win. Other names receiving votes included Mustangs, Missiles, and Moons.

NICE START

In 1966, Joe Auer returned the opening kickoff of the Dolphins' first game ever for a 95-yard touchdown against the Oakland Raiders.

LEFT: Bill Stanfill
ABOVE: Freddie Solomon

Talking Football

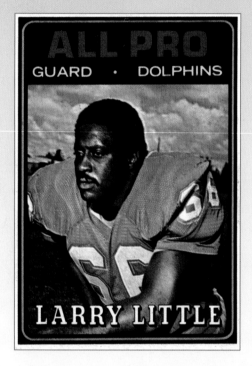

ALL PRO

GUARD · DOLPHINS

LARRY LITTLE

"I don't know any other way to lead but by example."

► **Don Shula,** *on his coaching style*

"To go 14–0 was great, but we all knew we could be knocked out any time, and we didn't want all that hard work to go for nothing."

► **Larry Little,** *on the pressure to win in the 1972 playoffs*

"I've always had great receivers. It's not just me doing it."

► **Dan Marino,** *on what it takes to be a record-setting quarterback*

"Any time you try to win everything, you must be willing to lose everything."

► **Larry Csonka,** *on taking chances and giving 100 percent*

"I'm a very nice guy. But when I put on the helmet, I change."

▶ *Jake Long, on being aggressive on the football field*

"He had us believing there was nothing we couldn't overcome."

▶ *Bob Griese, on Don Shula*

"My heart has always been in Miami."

▶ *Jason Taylor, on playing for the Dolphins three different times*

"I didn't take the highway here. I came the back way."

▶ *Cameron Wake, on his path to NFL stardom*

LEFT: Larry Little   **ABOVE**: Jake Long

Great Debates

People who root for the Dolphins love to compare their favorite moments, teams, and players. Some debates have been going on for years! How would you settle these classic football arguments?

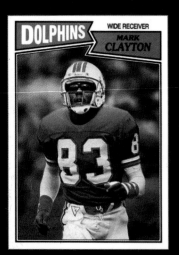

Mark Clayton was the Dolphins' greatest receiver ...

... because 20 years after he retired, he still held the team record with 550 catches. Clayton (   ) was Dan Marino's favorite target. He caught 50 or more passes six times and led the league in touchdowns twice. Without Clayton, Marino's passing statistics might have looked very different.

Numbers don't tell the whole story. Paul Warfield was the greatest ...

... because he used his blazing speed and sure hands to make catches—and make his teammates better. Warfield tied up two defenders on almost every play, which meant there were only nine men left to stop Miami's powerful running game. When the Dolphins threw the ball Warfield's way, he almost always made a big play. He averaged more than 21 yards a catch during his five seasons in Miami.

The No Name defense of the 1970s was Miami's best ....

... because that squad knew how to keep opponents out of the end zone. In 1973, the Dolphins held 11 teams to two touchdowns or fewer and allowed only 150 points during the regular season. In two playoff games and the Super Bowl, they gave up a total of just 33 points. And for the record, there were plenty of big names on the No Names—including Bill Stanfill, Manny Fernandez, Nick Buoniconti, Dick Anderson, and Jake Scott. All five were named All-Pro in 1973.

That was ancient history. The "Killer B's" of the 1980s were the best ....

... because they played at a time when the passing game was taking off. Miami was at its best in 1982. The Dolphins came within a couple of plays of being undefeated during the regular season. They intercepted a total of 10 passes in back-to-back playoff games. The Killer B's got their nickname because many of the players had names starting with the letter *B*—including Bob Baumhower (right), Kim Bokamper, Doug Betters, and Lyle and Glenn Blackwood.

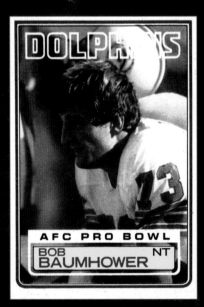

For the Record

T he great Dolphins teams and players have left their marks on the record books. These are the "best of the best" ...

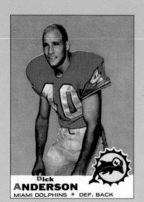

Dick Anderson

Troy Stradford

DOLPHINS AWARD WINNERS

WINNER	AWARD	YEAR
Don Shula	AFC Coach of the Year	1970
Don Shula	AFC Coach of the Year	1971
Don Shula	Coach of the Year	1972
Earl Morrall	Comeback Player of the Year	1972
Jake Scott	Super Bowl VII MVP	1973
Garo Yepremian	Pro Bowl MVP	1973
Dick Anderson	Defensive Player of the Year	1973
Larry Csonka	Super Bowl VIII MVP	1974
A.J. Duhe	Defensive Rookie of the Year*	1977
Larry Csonka	Comeback Player of the Year	1979
Doug Betters	Defensive Player of the Year	1983
Dan Marino	NFL Most Valuable Player	1984
Troy Stradford	Offensive Rookie of the Year	1987
Tim Bowens	Defensive Rookie of the Year	1994
Dan Marino	Comeback Player of the Year	1994
Ricky Williams	Pro Bowl MVP	2003
Brandon Marshall	Pro Bowl MVP	2012

The award given to the league's best first-year defensive player.

DOLPHINS ACHIEVEMENTS

ACHIEVEMENT	YEAR
AFC Champions	1971
AFC Champions	1972
Super Bowl VII Champions	1972*
AFC Champions	1973
Super Bowl VIII Champions	1973*
AFC East Champions	1974
AFC East Champions	1979
AFC East Champions	1981
AFC Champions	1982
AFC East Champions	1983
AFC Champions	1984
AFC East Champions	1985
AFC East Champions	1992
AFC East Champions	1994
AFC East Champions	2000
AFC East Champions	2001
AFC East Champions	2008

Super Bowls are played early the following year, but the game is counted as the championship of this season.

TOP: Tony Nathan was a star runner for the 1982 champs.
RIGHT: Bob Kuechenberg played in Miami's first four Super Bowls.
BELOW: This pennant celebrates the team's 1982 AFC title.

DOLPHINS

AFC PRO BOWL
BOB KUECHENBERG G

Pinpoints

The history of a football team is made up of many smaller stories. These stories take place all over the map—not just in the city a team calls "home." Match the pushpins on these maps to the **Team Facts**, and you will begin to see the story of the Dolphins unfold!

TEAM FACTS

1 Miami, Florida—*The Dolphins play their home games here.*

2 Springfield, Massachusetts—*Nick Buoniconti was born here.*

3 Grand River, Ohio—*Don Shula was born here.*

4 Pittsburgh, Pennsylvania—*Dan Marino was born here.*

5 Evansville, Indiana—*Bob Griese was born here.*

6 New Orleans, Louisiana—*A.J. Duhe was born here.*

7 Houston, Texas—*The Dolphins won Super Bowl VIII here.*

8 Los Angeles, California—*The Dolphins won Super Bowl VII here.*

9 Detroit, Michigan—*Jake Long was born here.*

10 Greenwood, South Carolina—*Jake Scott was born here.*

11 Tokyo, Japan—*The Dolphins played their second American Bowl* here.*

12 Larnaca, Cypress—*Garo Yepremian was born here.*

* The American Bowl was the annual NFL game played outside the United States.

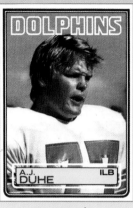

A.J. Duhe

Glossary

🧠 Football Words
🧠 Vocabulary Words

ALL-PRO—An honor given to the best players at their positions at the end of each season.

AMERICAN FOOTBALL CONFERENCE (AFC)—One of two groups of teams that make up the NFL.

AMERICAN FOOTBALL LEAGUE (AFL)—The football league that began play in 1960 and later merged with the NFL.

CANADIAN FOOTBALL LEAGUE (CFL)—A professional league in Canada that began play in 1958.

CONSISTENTLY—Doing something again and again at the same level of performance.

DIVERSITY—Variety or differences.

DIVISION—A group of teams that play in the same part of the country.

DOMINANT—Ruling or controlling.

DRAFT—The annual meeting during which NFL teams choose from a group of the best college players.

FIELD GOAL— A goal from the field, kicked over the crossbar and between the goal posts. A field goal is worth three points.

FUMBLES—Balls that are dropped by the players carrying them.

GENERATION—A period of years roughly equal to the time it takes for a person to be born, grow up, and have children.

HALL OF FAME—The museum in Canton, Ohio, where football's greatest players are honored.

INSPIRED—Gave positive and confident feelings to others.

INTERCEPTED—Caught in the air by a defensive player.

LATERAL—A toss of the ball backwards.

LOGO—A symbol or design that represents a company or team.

LUXURIOUS—Comfortable and elegant.

MOST VALUABLE PLAYER (MVP)—The award given each year to the league's best player; also given to the best player in the Super Bowl and Pro Bowl.

NATIONAL FOOTBALL LEAGUE (NFL)—The league that started in 1920 and is still operating today.

OVERTIME—The extra period played when a game is tied after 60 minutes.

PLAYOFFS—The games played after the regular season to determine which teams play in the Super Bowl.

POSTSEASON—The games played after the regular season, including the Super Bowl.

PRO BOWL—The NFL's all-star game, played after the regular season.

PROFESSIONAL—A player or team that plays a sport for money.

SACKS—Tackles of the quarterback behind the line of scrimmage.

SUPER BOWL—The championship of the NFL, played between the winners of the National Football Conference and American Football Conference.

OVERTIME

TEAM SPIRIT introduces a great way to stay up to date with your team! Visit our **OVERTIME** link and get connected to the latest and greatest updates. **OVERTIME** serves as a young reader's ticket to an exclusive web page—with more stories, fun facts, team records, and photos of the Dolphins. Content is updated during and after each season. The **OVERTIME** feature also enables readers to send comments and letters to the author! Log onto:

www.norwoodhousepress.com/library.aspx
and click on the tab: **TEAM SPIRIT** to access **OVERTIME**.

Read all the books in the series to learn more about professional sports. For a complete listing of the baseball, basketball, football, and hockey teams in the **TEAM SPIRIT** series, visit our website at:

www.norwoodhousepress.com/library.aspx

On the Road

MIAMI DOLPHINS
347 Don Shula Drive
Miami Gardens, Florida 33056
305-943-8000
www.miamidolphins.com

THE PRO FOOTBALL HALL OF FAME
2121 George Halas Drive NW
Canton, Ohio 44708
330-456-8207
www.profootballhof.com

On the Bookshelf

To learn more about the sport of football, look for these books at your library or bookstore:

- Frederick, Shane. *The Best of Everything Football Book.* North Mankato, Minnesota: Capstone Press, 2011.

- Jacobs, Greg. *The Everything Kids' Football Book: The All-Time Greats, Legendary Teams, Today's Superstars—And Tips on Playing Like a Pro.* Avon, Massachusetts: Adams Media Corporation, 2010.

- Editors of *Sports Illustrated for Kids. 1st and 10: Top 10 Lists of Everything in Football.* New York, New York: Sports Illustrated Books, 2011.

Index

About the Author

MARK STEWART has written more than 50 books on football and over 150 sports books for kids. He grew up in New York City during the 1960s rooting for the Giants and Jets, and was lucky enough to meet players from both teams. Mark comes from a family of writers. His grandfather was Sunday Editor of *The New York Times,* and his mother was Articles Editor of *Ladies' Home Journal* and *McCall's.* Mark has profiled hundreds of athletes over the past 25 years. He has also written several books about his native New York and New Jersey, his home today. Mark is a graduate of Duke University, with a degree in history. He lives and works in a home overlooking Sandy Hook, New Jersey. You can contact Mark through the Norwood House Press website.